Because we could not dance at the wedding

BECAUSE WE COULD NOT DANCE AT THE WEDDING

MICHAEL McKIMM

Michael McKimm was born in Belfast and grew up on the north Antrim coast. An Eric Gregory Award winner, he is the author of *Still This Need* (Heaventree Press, 2009) and *Fossil Sunshine* (Worple Press, 2013) and has edited two anthologies: *MAP: Poems After William Smith's Geological Map of 1815* (Worple Press, 2015) and *The Tree Line: Poems for Trees, Woods & People* (Worple Press, 2017). He lives in London.

for Zac

My quick sleep had deleted all
Of intervening time and place.
I only knew
The stay of your secure firm dry embrace.

Thom Gunn

Contents

First published in 2023 by
Worple Press
www.worplepress.co.uk

Printed by imprintdigital
Upton Pyne, Exeter
www.digital.imprint.co.uk

Typesetting and cover design by The Book Typesetters
hello@thebooktypesetters.com
07422 598 168
www.thebooktypesetters.com

ISBN 978-1-905208-49-4

Love Poem with Goshawk

It startled from behind a bank of earth

bird-shock black against twilight's burn
then unmistakeable by its low
pendulating glide between Scots pine
underfeathers like a shingle beach
those fizzing orange feet:

the something other   the quare fella
the shy and skulky   the beautiful
the wherehaveyoubeenallmylife
the nobleman   the sky dancer
the totem of the air   the breathy *gosh*

Because we could not dance at the wedding

– a *ceilidh*, designed for men and women,
not the usual disco in the dark –

the second you've one foot into the hushed
hotel room I take your right hand in my left,

place my other on your waist, and we move,
slowly, a waltz, three short steps between

the bed and wardrobe, a crisp turn
past the television. I've got you, you've

got me. Within a minute we work our way
up to a bebop, clumsy in the bathroom,

out again to the chest-of-drawers,
such a room you couldn't swing a cat in,

but you swing me and I laugh like tin pipes.
If they could see us now, half-cut on

smoky Ardbeg, exhausted, staggering,
my love we'd cause a sober brawl all right.

Earlier today I saw you from below,
as if through all the hymns and speeches

I was buried, grounded, my limbs
constricted – but now I'm level-headed

with your head, your waltzing eyes, your smile,
your breathing slow, deep, keeping time.

I have always believed in a god who dances.

To Go About

2005

What is this exhaustion – is it love?
Sleeping every day into the afternoon,
students back from lectures in the room above.
We wake into the single-bedded spoon
and lie like that, and doze, and sleep again
until the sky blues and sinks and thickens
and the low hum of commuter trains
calls us, ravenous, to the tempered kitchen.

Later, in the spring, we will find our pace,
up and out to the Common, the graveyard
on London Road, the river that will lace
illicit through the city. But caught off-guard
we'll take for now these dopey, limb-dead days,
body and arms awake in every way.

2006

Boys in thongs and short-shorts pass the barriers
throwing sweets and condoms and flirty looks
and drinks vouchers and then there's a guy in leather
on a lead and emos with full sleeve tattoos
and now the crowd is lost beneath the flag,
and after that march sailors, soldiers, police,
a samba band, the feathered Queens of Drag,
the Kings Cross Steelers, Leftfooters FC.

We drink it in, wide-eyed, edgy, nervous,
spectators only, a little lost at what to do
behind the railing. Then — pumped-up, agile, bravest —
you tug my shirt and find a clear way through:
we join the end, enjoy the summer sweat,
walking hand-in-hand down Oxford Street.

2007

Steam of breath, thick scarves and heavy duffels,
while braver couples plunge the bathing ponds.
Beyond black oaks the heath is muffled
in an auburn mist – we soldier on
and up, pensive, silent, a chill
on our cheeks, Christmas coming, time apart
with families. On Parliament Hill
we pluck place names like true London experts,
watch towers darkening with freckled lights.
We'd found that we could take the Silverlink
direct from our new bedsit flat.
But this year we've been stuck - I need a drink.
Descending, I pull loosely from your clutch,
uneasy at your brazen public touch.

2008

This walk will be our favourite for six years:
left out of the flat, past the Esso station,
through the churchyard with its broken graves,
Dagenham Brook, gypsy horses and alsatians,
a bridge above a road and railway docks,
across the Pitch and Putt to the wetlands:
sand martins, gadwall, kingfishers if in luck,
but mostly herons, moorhens, coots and swans.
Then Hackney Marsh, wind-carried football chants,
abandoned filter beds, a packed canal,
the slick boardwalk surveyed by cormorants
and a kestrel commanding the power-lines
where the long-horned cattle roam.
A pint perhaps, and then the same way home.

2011

How often will we stomp the riverbank,
timing it for our guests, hoping for sunshine,
allowing a stop (of course) to admire the flanks
of rowers cutting clean perpendicular lines?

The weeks are tightening like a drum:
the nerves, the suits, the fights, the food, the fuss.
The email from the friend who wouldn't come
but asked instead if he could pray for us.

But out here – where the rustle of the reeds
signals the barn, the whitewashed farmhouse,
our huge resilient chestnut tree –
all that disappears like the towing path in darkness.

Cows lolling on Christ Church Meadow, the wings of willow.
All the natural world just going with the flow.

2012

I lose you for a second, dodging tourists
on Piccadilly, then catch your determined
get-me-home-now back as it whisks
into Green Park station, two stairs at a time,
picking a queue wisely, Oyster ready
at the barrier, zipping left then right
to reach the escalator and the heady
heated hallway where approaching lights
shoot from the tunnel and we find our spot
for the perfect interchange, and we're on,
and breathe, and share your water bottle,
and get prepared to go when the doors re-open.
Always like this: full speed, hell-for-leather,
holding doors, finding seats, working together.

2013

Binoculars and camera are packed beside
the Ordnance Survey maps you've pinched off Bing,
the *Observer's Book of Trees*, a wildflower guide –
me quoting Longley: "tway blade, crowfoot, ling,
angelica" – the RSPB *Pocket Birds*
you bought me years ago.

The river peels from Bishop's Stortford,
narrowboats nudge into locks and a slow
procession of ramblers stop to rest their hips.
Not our style to walk with such a crowd.

Give us instead the drawn companionship
of a border-marking Angus herd
that follows us around the meadow's verge
as we seek out comfrey, goat rue, willowherb.

2014

Secret Water, from the Arthur Ransome book –
I must admit I thought we wouldn't make it:
first rail delays, and then how long it took
on the busy, curb-less road. But you'd not quit,
and I should have remembered
not just the days of planning but your need,
once the campfire's lit, to fan the embers:
the *Goblin* (gone), the Red Sea, Witch's Quay,
living footprints in actual, nearby sands.

So as we flip-flop round the tidal creek,
the mudflats, saltmarsh, grasslands, islands,
watching water play its hide-and-seek,
I remember why I'd thrown in my lot:
to "go about", to tie the bowline knot.

Conversion

2015

We're early so must be rescued
from the scrum of a waiting wedding
by the registrar, herself visibly relieved

that we're her Friday 4pm, ushering
us to the sanctuary of her office –
battered oakwood table with a recess

of red leather, an ancient Dell
which takes an age to start, box-files
on bracket shelves, a printer on a trolley.

We place on the table our proofs
of address, the certificate of our civil partnership;
she uses a bull-dog clip

to hold our passports open
and explains that she'll mostly just be typing
answers to her questions –

our names, our jobs, our fathers' names
and jobs, a verbal confirmation of address.
That's all it takes.

It's efficient and mundane.
But I realise I've not looked at you
since we sat down

and my heart is pounding, something I dismiss
to waiting rooms from childhood:
doctors, dentists, Boys' Brigade exams,

mornings in cold church halls,
lining up against reinforced glass
outside the Headmaster's office,

hoping you've done nothing wrong
and worried you'll be caught out anyway.
So that's what's playing on my mind

in this moment as the printer whirrs,
that someone's going to stop proceedings
(*It's A Criminal Offence To Defraud A Registrar*)

and sitting here, in this strange familiar room
with its ceiling tiles, you beside me in the plastic
chair you pull a little closer

in an unconscious modest movement,
I don't think I fully knew before
what language can do:

that the weight of our vows
is somehow writ larger now
is not something I thought I would admit.

She places it in front of us smiling
and hands me a fountain pen. You quickly check
the spelling and we sign.

What the River Carries

The river at the bottom of Grange Lane
    carries my earliest memories
all the way to the Lagan and the Irish Sea

    carries a certain summer heat and light
that's always there when I think about that place
    carries my brother fishing   catching his ear

on a fly-flung hook   and the form of a faceless
man   big man who thought he owned the lane
and didn't want us playing by the river

hearts thumping in our heads across the fields
    carries the fields   hot scuffed grass and horses
drinking from a water trough   rowan berries

floating in it   and our piss   carries the bass
the trout   the skiffly piddlers my brother
would catch   carries boulders and rounded pebbles

and water the colour of Belfast lemonade
    carries my first fumbles in the grass with R___
rubbing our crotches   until we were caught

(from then on I carried around a locked box)
    carries run-off from the Newtownabbey
quarries   carries old tyres   empty Tennent's cans

Crazy Prices woven carrier bags
    carries a dog we could not tame   my brother's
white drake   a full pet cemetery

    carries such a weight   sunshine and yellow dock
the avenue of greening trees   the horse putting
his long neck over the fence to take

the flat-palmed grass
     carries the removal van and old tea chests
(Where are you now R___?   Did we say goodbye?)

     carries on for fifty miles to meet the Lagan
somewhere west of Belfast   carries on through
farmland   scrubland   industrial estates   the backs

of houses   sometimes a bare trickle   sometimes
          reaching
even   above   the banks   carries spikes of hawthorn
     gorse flowers and heather

the sun always falling on it   carries on without me
     carries on for forty years   this river I carry
in a locked box   bursting with pure sunshine

Black Snow

grassfire – east London – 300 acres burned

To make fire requires a simple chemistry: heat, fuel, oxygen.

For heat read spark: dropped cigarette,
sun-pricked curve of broken bottle, our bodies as we fuck.

I walk through grass which is the fuel:
nest of skylark, meadow pipit, wisped bare kindling,

footballers sweating through Sunday fixtures and
what is now a field of ash, slick as a burned scalp

punctured with trees twisted like punked nudes
by Egon Schiele. *Bodies have their own light,*

he wrote, *which they consume to live: they burn.*
I step out onto this black snow and feel

your skin in the fullness of heat,
could hold you forever against these drifts of black.

Such heat in tiny things: dropped cigarette,
sun-pricked curve of broken bottle, our bodies as we fuck,

your hand in mine, the thermal that the buzzard rides
in the air that holds the smoke like a mist-net

which is the oxygen, which is what we breathe.

From the Kitchen Window

A road, a mile of kingdom – Patrick Kavanagh

i.

Best in winter light, winter gone on so long
and now long morning shadows falling on the almshouse
falling through the trees like splayed hands.

My own hands in last night's dishes
hurrying towards the last fork, mind
on route to the bus, emails, the day ahead.

And the day is opening from the east
behind me as winter light that climbs
quickly down the buildings sets alight
the horse chestnut and now – quick spirit –
casts in gold the skyscrapers at Stratford.
The sky is full and a little flustered.

I've missed the bus. My hands are full of forks.
I see the trees startling in their winter skeletons
each backlit by glass reflections
some pinpoint black, some full of flash.
Poplar, chestnut, cherry, maple, ash.

ii.

Sunlight is falling on frost on the roof of the almshouse.

I watch it from the kitchen, burning a cold yellow glow
on the ice-thatched tiles, then, as the sun rises, its reach

is lowered down the single-storey walls, bouncing back
off white paint and the gabled, quartered windows.

The workmen are going in and out with tools and planks
     of wood.
A woman has died and they're gutting it out for the next one.

The light hits the bottom of the wall and spreads towards me
across the narrow concrete apron, the strip of grass.

iii.

It has been the strangest noise
and I can't remember the first time
hearing it, a cockerel crowing
loud and clear from somewhere across the railway lines,
from someone's back garden in Earlham Grove,
a cockerel in the city.
                              And the almshouse
with its single-storey, gable end, pitched roof
could almost be a cowshed and on days like this,
a thick fog on the horizon, skyscrapers rubbed out,
the line of trees that skirt the school yard black
and bare like a belt of woodland

you could forget where you are, travel time
like a stone skimmed lightly on a lake
St. Paul's in the distance, chimneys
coking on the Lee canal.

Looking through the grey I see
small scrapings of poultry
and a good man imagining heaven:
single-storey, white gable, pitched roof.

iv.

To look at the world and pause it once each day
to hold it like this brightening Sunday morning
just back from the pool and catching up on dishes
my hands cracked and dried, turning the sponge
in a glass and glancing up to see the oldest lady
from the almshouse with her son, moving slow
on her stick, huge yellow hat the trumpet
of a daffodil, her son with her hand hooked in his arm
her mouth moving – she's chatting to him – all the way
down the path, through the gate, into the car
and smiling up as he puts his hand
upon her head the way a policeman might
and the car slowly safely pulls away.

V.

The window has made me late again, big crow
on the satellite dish beaking south from the almshouse
wet morning in May, the sky tall and white
tree blossom all over the road, cars sluicing like velcro
man on the radio saying I am of windrush
no regrets, I came from windrush, no regrets
and all of these people I know so well
man in a blazer with red handkerchief
twin boys with umbrellas webbed with spiderman
the mum and little girl always running late
always smiling
the TA in his oversized suit, head down
barely out of school himself, cute guy
whose head is swinging through his earphones
the girls who talk behind their hands
because everything is crack-up-funny
all these people who've left whatever homes
they have this morning, heading out into the rain.

vi.

The heatwave has broken momentarily
breeze through the kitchen window
thin chalk of distant clouds
but still no rain: the stripped lilac is bent
and brown, the roses sag burnt pink
the light off the almshouse walls is sharp as sulphur.

Even now we are amazed by the seasons'
sweeping unfamiliarity
country we think we know so well
stunned in this element of surprise: packed
beaches, moorland fires, a penalty shootout
in some suddenly not so foreign land.

People are passing in short sleeves and shades
and slip on shoes, so used to this now
they've perfected the slow low bovine
walk of summer;
a man drinks from a pint of milk;
a toddler runs in a batman swimsuit
armbands already inflated on his skinny arms
even this far from the pool.

Give me a chance today
to let the world in:
cars unparking in the street, the radio with its catch
of common fisheries, the latest boat to sink
off Libya, the this is what the people
voted for, the dishes soaped like oil
in the sunlight, the stroll to the bus stop
the hint and hope that a storm might come
just momentarily might.

vii.

The radio is on but I've not been listening
I've not thought about the news for at least two minutes
and there's a plane spraying a rope of white
across the growing blue, and behind the chestnut trees
the Manhattan Loft Apartments burn russet
gold in the sunlight, tallest of the muddle of Stratford
a thousand windows looking back at me
and I've not thought about the news
for at least three minutes

viii.

Today again the light comes as a gift.

I turn to find the bedroom door ajar
the gentle splashing of my husband soaping
in the shower, the bright sun
from the bathroom window warm
on my face. I smile.

I've slept an hour.
All night sharp as a clock, thoughts
on replay like a jukebox.

I roll toward the curtains, heat
behind them, light lining the edges
cutting the middle where folds
don't quite meet.

The whole room is lit by softness
calling me out of the covers
two feet on the floor.

In the kitchen I raise the blind
slow as an eclipse
light breaking under black
spreading in a band across the sink
the work surface, rising up the walls
my chest, my neck, my mouth, my eyes

that see the road, the trees
the almshouse and the sky.

Romford Road and Broadway

All year there have been roadworks in the town centre,
returning the traffic to two-way, carving lovely snakes
of cycle lanes, slotting slabs
of black and quartz-grey granite into widened footpaths.
It's almost done. And now, on this cold
October morning stopped at the lights on my way to work
I watch from the top deck of the bus a man in overalls
and thick green boots power-hosing the pavement,
firing a focused jet into the little grouty
avenues between the polished stones.
Is there any job in the world more satisfying?
His back is straight, his head is bent just slightly, his arms
out in front holding the metal pipe like a scythe or a
        broadfork,
the thick yellow hose coiled behind him
and the water shooting through
a good half metre reach before it hits
the ground and flares out like a paper fan –
all its energy concentrated in a core
no bigger than a two-pound coin, unhooking gum
and leaves and cigarette butts and the brown sludge
and black grease that's already trodden down upon
the new street, a crisp dividing line between his clean slate
and the remaining ground to come, and all the run-off
like a sudden spring with thin escaping tributaries
filling left and right between the blocks
like marbles in a marble-maze. He meets the kerb
and takes a forward step, no break in his flow,
works crab-wise at a steady pace – and does he see
each stone in turn alone, to finish this one before the next,
or does he have in his mind's eye a foot-wide trench
he's digging in a hungry parallel, or does he see as I see now
a harvest-ready field that he must cut
in tidy swathes, close and sharp as possible at the root?
He's probably already clocking how much time
he'll need to clear this ordered zone between the Nando's

and the traffic lights and how long from there
to get to his next job this afternoon, and how long then
'til he gets home... but I swear
I see a smile across his face as each new layer
gives way to show another patch come clean.
Is there anything in the world
more satisfying? To feel the pressure
in your arms, the tremor through your well-placed feet,
to catch the earth by force and make it gleam.

Love Poem with Beech Coppard

Another heavy night,
the endless freight trains speeding past
and curtains leaking light...
I try to think of the beechmast

we collected in the woods
on Saturday: those little shells
which crackled underfoot,
the tiny three-edged nut they held

so tight... But wake again...
And so I start to grow around
our room a veteran
of beech, the coppice from the ground

to nest our bodies, heads,
then a claw of ancient pollard
encircling the bed.
And while you sleep so fast and hard

I will attend the tree,
for birds, black beetles, bats, and keep
the dead wood turned, and see
it safe in storm. I too might sleep,

for what else but a crown
of thickset branches could protect
our limbs, grown so well known
that with a hug you now detect

this woodland I've conceived –
and pull me in against the fight,
to dream in just the leaves,
just woodland noise and woodland light.

Poem for one whose birthday falls in winter

Swimming and dreaming were becoming indistinguishable – Roger Deakin

How often love do these poems start in bed
awake   awakening   the dark   the half-dreamed thread
of future life   or wish   or memory?

Today I pull the duvet up like a warm soft sun
    a deserted beach in Kent   our anniversary
thirty degrees   stripping casually as a Swede
    inching down the hard tanned stones
to the lip of water   warm as a well-drawn bath

Breaststroking   front crawling   groyne jumping   quick feed
quick dry   back in   hand-plunging   your buoyant head-
        thrown laugh

Out there it's January
it's cold
the alarm's about to go

I turn   and dip   and put my arms around you…
we sink we float   Let's float a little longer…

Ah this bed   this gentle bed of water

What the greenfinch actually sounds like

Tree at my window, window tree – Robert Frost

I hoover the dust off some 4kg dumbbells, find exercises
    online and set to
in front of an upstairs window. *Goblet squat. Bent-over row.*
    Cross body hammer curl.
Lateral raise. I watch our neighbour's cat disappear below
    the fence-line.

★

We hear a song like a winnowing hinge and follow it
    through the gorse,
finding a greenfinch calling from a bramble. Butterflies
    everywhere we turn.
We look them up when we get home: speckledwood,
    orange tip, brimstone.

★

I listen to Beast Mode on Spotify as I lift the dumbbells,
    right arm first for ten, then left,
then repeat. A bumblebee as big as the phalanx of a thumb
    dozes up to the window,
bounces off the glass a few times and drifts away. The horse
    chestnut has electric neon leaves.

★

We come across a swathe still reeling from the grassfire two
    years back. Black, tormented,
clawing at the sky. I begin to collect favourite trees: the oak
    in Bush Wood that sits alone
where three paths meet, its branches low and long and
    scoring the air like lightning.

★

What the greenfinch actually sounds like is a single cicada
 placed deep in a tree, its hot rattling rasp
slowed and elongated to a creaking purr. Or a cow box toy
 turning out a lackadaisical moo,
beginning with some momentum then petering off with a
 shrug of exhaustion.

★

In a knuckle of woods a slatted garage door painted with
 foot high bubble letters:
THE WOODS ARE LOVELY, DARK AND DEEP, BUT
 I HAVE PROMISES TO KEEP.
I go through nettles and Spanish bluebells to take a photo.
 Miles to go before we sleep.

★

Droplets static on the window, nudged from their
 fastenings by the newly fallen, slip
like tadpoles down the pane, chicane through bubbles of
 their sister-spawn. A crow glosses
the chimney tops. The world is more silent than ever in
 this cocoon of cloud and water.

★

Sun flares off the taut white skin of the temporary morgue
 which sits there in the woods
like a wedding marquee. We are stopped in our tracks by
 parabolas of sunlight spellbound with spores
of bulrush and dandelion and who knows what fairy dust
 floating and dancing softly through the air.

★

Some sort of warblers gossiping in the hawthorn, shopping
       around for evening snacks and furnishings.
I have a vision of my mum and Auntie Margaret in Marks
       & Sparks, picking things up and
putting them down again, their conversation unbroken and
       overlapping and untroubled by time.

★

I watch our neighbour's cat settle down like a small loaf to
       bake in the sun.
The conkers are coming already. Little spiny balls. Neon
       green. They look like virus particles.
What the greenfinch actually sounds like: grating nutmeg;
       sharpening a rusty knife.

March – June 2020

Low Traffic Neighbourhood

Because our Council is planting thyme
in boxes to stop traffic

and on raised beds
in unused parking spaces

there are all these scraggly painted signs
that say *Please Take Our Thyme*.

and our mint and rosemary and please
water us and please take only what you need.

You're gliding on your bicycle
and I'm just about keeping pace

on foot, every so often
doing a two-step at the curb

where the sun is kissing my heels
in a puddle reflecting the rowan trees.

Oh what a life!
Trying to keep up with your husband

on a buried street
watching him whizz off to get the oven on

while you ponder at chives and sage
and a spoke of lovage gifted by a stranger.

Tattoo

June 2021: NHS blood service rules change to end discrimination against gay and bisexual men giving blood

I wish our friends knew more about our anger.

Today, the world, the sky,
damp humid June, roof tiles
brown as leather,
there's a plant that's sprung up
in our neighbour's garden
some sort of *salvia*
scab-red petals
inked with a faint black smudge.
I sponge a glass in the sink
and watch the soft rain
make grass greener.

My husband has just gone out
to give blood for the first time
and he's gone out angry.

He read in a survey how many
people in this country
still think he shouldn't be allowed to.

He's gone out angry to give them
his beautiful blood.

Maybe, he said, they should be made
to sign forms
to consent
to receive the blood
of a gay man.

And maybe
if they refuse
they should die.

No, he said, turning, no.
Not die,

before he closed the door.

Our home is left in sudden silence.
Magpie-cackle, slow hum
and occasional bleat of traffic.
I look out at the red-pecked plant
and breathe a little
at the relief of space and silence
bloody angry myself
at the turning trick of temper.

I imagine him cycling down Forest Lane,
headphones in, that anger doing-
What now? : I don't know : maybe
already out of his head,
the mind taken by the distraction of the *now*:
school-run, music, people in the street,
the sheen on the road.

Later, when he comes home
smiling, sugared on orange squash
and digestive biscuits,
a sticker on his bike helmet
(two hearts like on a sailor's arm)
gushing about the nurse who said he had
good flow
and jumped for joy
when he told her he was gay
he'll tell me again how he came to have
that unfledged anger

how his parents who had always gone up to give blood,
regularly marching –
I imagine them marching,
and always up, one never
goes down to do a good thing –

practiced, perfunctory,
sleeves rolled, swab and pierce and *go*,
simple as communion,
or filling the tank,
or watering the plants –

how they asked him when he turned eighteen,
as they had asked their two older sons,
Right then,
are you coming to give blood?

How he'd blushed
and busied himself
at the dishes,
or pretended
to be taking something
to his room
and said breezily enough

No
No, I can't, I'm
I've

I got a tattoo

Eighteen. Why is it I feel
his anger
like a needle?

Hellfire and brimstone? No, not that.
Bookish-class shrug? Not that either.

A letting go.
A loss.

We'd all have done things differently
would we not?

     I remember when my brother dyed his hair
     that rinsed, slush-puppy red,
     all this thundering movement on the stairs
     my father practically throwing him up the stairs
     to his knees over the bath under the faucet –
     the most violent thing I saw in our house, ever.
     All that colour running into the plughole,
     red blemishes like bruises for weeks on the cork tiles.

     No regrets
     is the greatest lie I've heard.

That same night
cut on cider with his friends in South Park
after a few at the Dyke and Dog

home to his parents watching television,
a glass of water at the sink
and

Well, he said, the truth is I am

gay

and I can't give blood.
It's against the law.

There is a way to enfranchise your children
but I wish that way did not breed latent
anger

I wish that anger wasn't
needled deep

I wish our friends knew more about our anger

that we did not hold it from them
in the shrug and sleepy smile

of relative peace.

My husband's tattoo is the shape
of a jigsaw piece,
low on his hip,
about two inches squared.
Four loops curled as sea-worked coves.
Purplish now, black jeans faded at the knees.

I never can tell
whether it's a piece of him that's missing
or if this is the only piece,
and the rest of the puzzle
is waiting to be found.

Later on he'll tell me about his blood type
and that he's passed his screening
and that his donation has been issued
to University Hospital Norwich.

I am looking out the window
at the strange, exotic flowers,
their tangle of stems, red and black
coagulating on the petals.

Every now and then, simply the world,
the neighbour's garden, the people
on the street, the plants, the tiles,
the soft rain.

Bicep curl. Overhead press. Small movements in the horse
     chestnut flick to the fence:
a wren no bigger than a walnut, tail like a shoe-horn in the
     heel of a clog, its irrefutable song
spinning out across the gardens. A daily needling that I
     should feel luckier or sadder or more afraid.

★

I dream an indoor swimming pool filled by a melting
     glacier and wake
with what I guess you'd call survivor's guilt. How still the
     pool must be now.
To paraphrase Robert Hass: maybe you need to write a
     poem about guilt.

★

Looping west round Shoulder of Mutton Pond to gobby
     birdsong, flustered leaves
and shadows darting across the path. Blackcaps. We study
     them through binoculars,
their scuffed punk hairdos like they've also taken the
     clippers to themselves.

★

Horse chestnut flowers blow in through the window and
     land at my feet
as I lift the weights, a fine sweet scent, white petals with
     pink swirls like raspberry-ripple.
Maybe you need to write a poem about gratitude.

★

Every now and then the distraction of the sky.

But I don't want the world to get away with this today.

I'll ask him about the *salvia*
and he'll come to join me at the window.
Our neighbour's garden is wild as the hills.
We'll look at the petals red as strawberries

but I don't want them, I don't
want their plush soft distraction. Not today.

Heatwave

Rain in the night.
        Comes with the wind like bucket
after bucket of shingle on the flat roof
you hugging me from behind in the half-sleep
"Do you hear it?"   as if rain should warrant
such a question, awaken
us from dreams tautened
like stretched strings, cooling wires
could wash the knotted naked heat
that has kept us feverish for weeks, rain
remembered from childhood:
belting horizontally in draughts as if the sea
had slapped its hand across the window.

Sound is no proof: we have to look.
Silently we clamber from the bed
move the curtain like a hinge
through which we pull
the streetlamp's showerhead, pavements
black as jet, creeks running kerbstones
frothing drains, early drivers
going slow, their wipers flicking seismographs.

We are close to the glass, hunkered down
to hide our nakedness. The rain thumps
off a wheelie-bin. It's like one of those nights
when we started out, cold-broke and up late
by the opened window, the font of the world
erratic and illegible, the hot new streets
the silence and the strength we drew from it.
You light a cigarette. I sip a G&T—

which was when I woke and saw that it
was dream, my buttress limbs
your solid sleep, your back to mine
my forehead thick with sweat. But not

2010

In Paris I feel suddenly old, or wise,
lying awake in the hostel near Bastille,
teenagers pounding corridors, the weight of lies
of my own youth.
                              A judder in the keel:
our wedding plans, my autumn in the States.

It is too hot, but you coax me down
to share the narrow bottom bunk, too late
to worry about sleep – better to plan
the day's itinerary: Jardin
de Luxembourg, Boulevard St. Michel,
and into the dark of the catacombs.
Towering skulls: not a vision of some hell
but a careful tomb, neat and organised,
loved ones, where they could be, laid side by side.

2009

Separate beds: me in my old room
where the heating clanks, you in my brother's
which gets the early morning sun
even in March and has the ivy all a-bother
with birds, so you've been awake for hours
when I bring you a cup of tea,
not sure if you should go to get your shower
or wait for me to give you the all clear.

Later we'll head west one hundred miles,
watch basalt yield to limestone on the drive
along the coast towards wind-wrecked Malin,
my parents sure that nothing's done by halves,
you'll see it all – no walks, just car-seat range –
but we will smile throughout this small sea change.

Acknowledgements

I am grateful to the editors of the following publications where some of these poems originally appeared: *fourteen poems, Impossible Archetype, Poetry Wales, The Tangerine, Twin Skies: Poems from Cork & Coventry* (O'Bheal Press, 2021). Parts of 'What the greenfinch actually sounds like' appeared in *Arrival at Elsewhere* (Against the Grain Press, 2020) curated by Carl Griffin in aid of NHS Charities Together.

A number of these poems were published in *Queering the Green: Post-2000 Queer Irish Poetry* (Lifeboat Press, 2021) – my thanks to its editor Paul Maddern for including me, which helped shape this book in my mind. Thanks again to Paul and also to Zoë Brigley for their kind words about the collection, and to Birk Thomassen for the beautiful cover image.

The epigraphs are taken from the following sources: Thom Gunn, 'The Hug', *The Man with Night Sweats* (Faber, 2002); Patrick Kavanagh, 'Inniskeen Road: July Evening', *Ploughman and Other Poems* (Macmillan & Co., 1936); Roger Deakin, *Waterlog* (Chatto & Windus, 1999); Robert Frost, 'Tree at My Window', *West-Running Brook* (Henry Holt & Co., 1928).

I am grateful to Luigi Coppola and John Freeman for advice and encouragement with early drafts of poems over many years.

A huge thank you to Peter Carpenter for his friendship, his belief in these poems, and for nurturing this collection with his generous and careful editing.

Finally, thanks as always to Zachary Lamdin – more than word can wield the matter.

Love Poem with Sanderling

Love   I
                        sing
                                          of sanderling
                        quicketyquickety
                                          sanderlinging

over pebbles –
                        white
                                          as moon
            and graphite beaked –
                        little sandplough

singing back to us
                        across the knuckle
                                          -frozen estuary
            its Arctic morse:

hold me close now

                                    hold me close
                  slowly
                              slowly

                                                sander
                  linger

Daffodils

The Council in its frugal simple stealth
planted them last autumn, those green
and high-viz volunteers pushing little
mines into leaf-flat mud, and now as if
a switch was flicked they've detonated
all over roundabouts, along the sides
of roads, on brick-raised strips of grass
that cushion the estates – blocks and bands
and concertinas, yin and yang and shooting
stars, trailblazers brightening the feet
of lampposts, there to catch the winter-weary
cold bus window eye with the joyful
wild and singular announcement *This Is Spring*

flooding like a river through the churchyard
thick as a wheat field in West Ham Park
snow-survivors reaching heads up to the trees
with a raucous here we are we made it please make room
we are the sunshine fallen from the sky, we are
the darkness let to bloom.

amen, to cast
my runes at last and place
with care, to look at these three
looking at the game –
together – and to know it isn't
luck, it isn't only luck.

Rummikub in Co. Antrim

My dad rearranges
postage stamp tiles
so they face the same way
on the small coffee table
in the garden at Carnkirk,
this rare day we can sit

outside – no drop of wind –
and both my mum and I
are yet to go down, my pieces
spilling off the rack
and hardly hidden, and Zac
is running away with it

connecting colours
and numbers with a focused
swoop of his eyes
and fingers busy as flies,
so mum is sighing
and putting her head in her hands

and dad is laughing
and saying we've got some
competition here – and I am so
stuck and adrift
I'm looking across at the sea
and beaten rocks

and thinking of prayer.
For mine was a basalt prayer
for the hundred ways it could have gone,
dark and hot and troubled
even now, a prayer I need
to close with a black

Aubade

Sometimes when we wake
and stir and turn and sleep again
rolled up like a carpet

there will be a rhythm coming
through the deep:
the tapping of your toe upon

the curled back of my feet.
A tapping I will waken to a code
with a dozed hand

that's reached across your chest
by matching with my thumb
your dancing, dreamy notes.

So you'll beat then a tap tap tap
like a woodpecker would
on my sole's gnarled wood

which I mimic in our practised way
before I play across your front
a tappity bodhrán flick

which your toes kick out quick.
No matter how long we've improvised
this irregular, attuned

surprise, this gentle sesh, this jam
I never know what rhyme you'll send
what restless telegram to say

are you now ready for the day?

entirely dream: I still feel your hug
and hear your question, slumber-drugged
with smiles, and know from the wet ground
how our two nights intertwined.